Prayers That Avail Much®
for Moms

James 5:16

by
Germaine Copeland

And this is the confidence that we have in him, that, if we ask any thing according to his will, he heareth us: and if we know that he hear us, whatsoever we ask, we know that we have the petitions that we desired of him.

1 John 5:14,15

Harrison House
Tulsa, Oklahoma

08 07 06 05 04   10 9 8 7 6 5 4 3 2 1

Prayers That Avail Much® for Moms
Pocket Edition
ISBN 1-57794-641-3
Copyright © 2004 by Germaine Copeland
38 Sloan St.
Roswell, GA 30075

Published by **Harrison House, Inc.**
P.O. Box 35035
Tulsa, Oklahoma 74153

Contents

Introduction

Prayers That Avail Much® for Moms was created and designed for you because you are important to your family and your Heavenly Father. Because you face more complex situations and lead a vastly different life than your mother did when she was raising you, the stress of being a mother has also increased. You, as a mom, affect more than just your family — you are helping shape generations. Such a task is not accomplished successfully without help and love from a close adviser. The prayers in this book will strengthen you spiritually, physically, and emotionally and are designed for your daily use. I encourage you to read God's Word and pray these Scriptural prayers. Being a godly mother today involves more than rearing children and managing a household — it is fulfilling your destiny. You were born for such a time as this. Your children shall rise up and call you blessed.

—Germaine Copeland, President
Word Ministries, Inc.

Personal Confessions

Jesus is Lord over my spirit, my soul, and my body (Phil. 2:9-11).

Jesus has been made unto me wisdom, righteousness, sanctification, and redemption. I can do all things through Christ Who strengthens me (1 Cor. 1:30; Phil. 4:13).

The Lord is my shepherd. I do not want. My God supplies all my need according to His riches in glory in Christ Jesus (Ps. 23; Phil. 4:19).

I do not fret or have anxiety about anything. I do not have a care (Phil. 4:6; 1 Pet. 5:6,7).

I am the Body of Christ. I am redeemed from the curse, because Jesus bore my sicknesses and carried my diseases in His own body. By His stripes I am healed. I forbid any sickness or disease to operate in my body. Every organ and tissue of my body functions in the perfection in which God created it to function. I honor God and bring glory to Him in my body (Gal. 3:13; Matt. 8:17; 1 Pet. 2:24; 1 Cor. 6:20).

I have the mind of Christ and hold the thoughts, feelings, and purposes of His heart (1 Cor. 2:16).

I am a believer and not a doubter. I hold fast to my confession of faith. I decide to walk by faith and practice faith. My faith comes by hearing and hearing by the Word of God. Jesus is the author and the developer of my faith (Heb. 4:14; Heb. 11:6; Rom. 10:17; Heb. 12:2).

The Holy Spirit has shed the love of God abroad in my heart, and His love abides in me richly. I keep myself in the Kingdom of light, in love, in the Word; and the wicked one touches me not (Rom. 5:5; 1 John 4:16; 1 John 5:18).

I tread upon serpents and scorpions and over all the power of the enemy. I take my shield of faith and quench his every fiery dart. Greater is He Who is in me than he who is in the world (Ps. 91:13; Eph. 6:16; 1 John 4:4).

I am delivered from this present evil world. I am seated with Christ in heavenly places. I reside in the Kingdom of God's dear Son. The law of the Spirit of life in Christ Jesus has made me free from the law of sin and death (Gal. 1:4; Eph. 2:6; Col. 1:13; Rom. 8:2).

I fear not, for God has given me a spirit of power, of love, and of a sound mind. God is on my side (2 Tim. 1:7; Rom. 8:31).

I hear the voice of the Good Shepherd. I hear my Father's voice, and the voice of a stranger I will not follow. I roll my works upon the Lord. I commit and trust them wholly to Him. He will cause my thoughts to become agreeable to His will, and so shall my plans be established and succeed (John 10:27; Prov. 16:3).

I am a world-overcomer because I am born of God. I represent the Father and Jesus well. I am a useful member in the Body of Christ. I am His workmanship re-created in Christ Jesus. My Father God is all the while effectually at work in me both to will and do His good pleasure (1 John 5:4,5; Eph. 2:10; Phil. 2:13).

I let the Word dwell in me richly. He Who began a good work in me will continue until the day of Christ (Col. 3:16; Phil. 1:6).

1

To Walk in the Word

Father, in the name of Jesus, I make a commitment to walk in the Word. Your Word living in me produces Your life in this world. Your Word is integrity itself, and I trust my life to its provisions.

You have sent Your Word forth into my heart. It dwells in me richly in all wisdom, and I meditate in it day and night so that I may diligently act on it. The Incorruptible Seed is abiding in my spirit, growing mightily in me now, producing Your nature, Your life. It is my counsel, my shield, my buckler, my powerful weapon in battle. The Word is a lamp to my feet and a light to my path, making my way plain before me. I do not stumble, for my steps are ordered in the Word.

The Holy Spirit leads and guides me into all the truth. He gives me understanding, discernment, and comprehension so that I am preserved from the snares of the evil one.

I delight myself in You and Your Word, and You put Your desires within my heart. I commit my way unto You, and You bring it to pass. I am confident that You are at work in me now both to will and to do all Your good pleasure.

I exalt Your Word, hold it in high esteem, and give it first place. I make my schedule around Your Word. Your Word is final authority, settling all questions that confront me. I agree with the Word of God, and I disagree with any thoughts, conditions, or circumstances contrary to Your Word. I boldly and confidently say that my heart is fixed and established on the solid foundation — the living Word of God!

Scripture References

Psalms 37:4,5,23; 91:4;
   112:7,8; 119:105
Hebrews 4:12
Colossians 1:9; 3:16; 4:2
Joshua 1:8
1 Peter 1:23; 3:12

John 16:13
Ephesians 6:10
Luke 18:1
Philippians 2:13
2 Corinthians 10:5

2

To Put on the Armor of God

In the name of Jesus, I put on the whole
armor of God, that I may be able to stand
against the wiles of the devil.

I take unto myself the whole armor of God
that I may be able to withstand in the evil day
and, having done all, to stand. I stand, therefore,
having my loins girt about with truth. Your
Word, Lord, is truth, containing all the weapons
of my warfare, which are not carnal, but mighty
through God to the pulling down of strongholds.

I have on the breastplate of righteousness,
which is faith and love. My feet are shod with
the preparation of the Gospel of peace. In
Christ Jesus I have peace and pursue peace with
all men. I am a minister of reconciliation,
proclaiming the good news of the Gospel.

I take the shield of faith, wherewith I am able to quench all the fiery darts of the wicked, the helmet of salvation (holding the thoughts, feelings, and purposes of God's heart), and the sword of the Spirit, which is the Word of God. In the face of all trials, tests, temptations, and tribulation, I cut to pieces the snare of the enemy by speaking the Word of God. Greater is He that is in me than he that is in the world.

Thank You, Father, for the armor. I will pray at all times — on every occasion, in every season — in the Spirit, with all [manner of] prayer and entreaty. To that end I will keep alert and watch with strong purpose and perseverance, interceding in behalf of my children and all the saints. My power, ability, and sufficiency are from You, Who has qualified me as a minister and a dispenser of a new covenant [of salvation through Christ]. Amen.

Scripture References

Ephesians 2:14; 6:11-14	2 Corinthians 5:18; 10:4
Ephesians 6:14-17 AMP	2 Corinthians 3:5,6 AMP
John 17:17	1 John 4:4
Psalm 34:14	

3

To Glorify God

Father, in view of Your mercy, I offer my body as a living sacrifice, holy and pleasing to You — this is my spiritual act of worship. It is [not in my own strength], for You are all the while effectually at work in me — energizing and creating in me the power and desire — both to will and work for Your good pleasure.

Father, I will not draw back in fear, for then Your soul would have no pleasure in me. I was bought for a price, made Your very own. So, I honor You and bring glory to You in my body.

I called on You in the day of trouble; You delivered me, and I shall honor and glorify You. I rejoice because You delivered me and drew me to Yourself out of the control and dominion of darkness and transferred me into the Kingdom of the Son of Your love. I will confess and praise

You, O Lord my God, with my whole (united) heart; and I will glorify Your name for evermore.

As a bond servant of Jesus Christ, I receive and develop the talents You have given me, for I would have You say of me, "Well done, you upright (honorable, admirable) and faithful servant!" I make use of the gifts (faculties, talents, qualities) according to the grace given me. I let my light so shine before men that they may see my moral excellence and my praise-worthy, noble, and good deeds, and recognize, honor, praise, and glorify You, my Father.

In Jesus' name, my life lovingly expresses truth in all things — speaking truly, dealing truly, living truly. Whatever I do — no matter what it is — in word or deed, I do everything in the name of the Lord Jesus and in [dependence upon] His Person, giving praise to God the Father through Him. Whatever my task, I work at it heartily (from the soul), as [something done] for the Lord and not for men. To God be all glory and honor and praise. Amen.

Scripture References (AMP)

Romans 12:1,6	Psalms 50:15; 86:12
Philippians 2:13	Colossians 1:13; 3:17,23
Hebrews 10:38	Matthew 5:16; 25:21
1 Corinthians 6:20	Ephesians 4:15

4

To Be God-Inside Minded

I am a spirit learning to live in a natural world. I have a soul, and I live in a physical body. I am in the world, but not of the world. God of peace, I ask You to sanctify me in every way; to keep my whole spirit, soul, and body blameless until that day when our Lord Jesus Christ comes again. Father, You called me, and You are completely dependable. You said it, and You will do this. Thank You for the Spirit Who guides me into all truth through my regenerated human spirit.

Lord, Your searchlight penetrates my human spirit, exposing every hidden motive. You actually gave me Your Spirit so I can know the wonderful things You have given us. I am a child of God — born of, filled with, and led by the Spirit of God. I listen to my heart as I look to the Spirit inside me. Thank You, Holy Spirit, for directing me and illuminating my mind. By an inward witness, You lead me in the way I should go in all the affairs of life. The eyes of my understanding are being enlightened. Wisdom is in my inward parts. Your love is perfected in me.

Father, I walk not after the flesh, but after the spirit. I listen to and obey the voice of my spirit, which is controlled by the Holy Spirit. I examine my leading in the light of the Word. I trust in You, Lord, with all of my heart and lean not to my own understanding. In all of my ways I acknowledge You, and You direct my paths.

Holy Spirit, You are my Counselor, teaching me to educate, train, and develop my human spirit. The Word of God shall not depart out of my mouth. I meditate therein day and night. My way shall be prosperous, and I will have good success in life. I am a doer of the Word and put Your Word first.

Scripture References

1 Thessalonians 5:23,24	Ephesians 1:18; 5:18
John 3:6,7; 14:26; 16:13	Isaiah 48:17
Proverbs 3:5,6 KJV;	1 John 2:20; 4:12
20:27 NLT	Psalm 119:105
1 Corinthians 2:12 NLT	Joshua 1:8
Romans 8:1,14,16	James 1:22

5

To Rejoice in the Lord

My Lord, this is the day that You have made.
I rejoice and am glad in it! I rejoice in You
always. I delight myself in You, Lord. Happy
am I because God is my Lord!

Father, You love me and rejoice over me with
joy. Hallelujah! I am redeemed. I come with
singing, and everlasting joy is upon my head. I
obtain joy and gladness, and sorrow and sighing
flee away. That spirit of rejoicing, joy, and
laughter is my heritage. Where the Spirit of the
Lord is there is liberty — emancipation from
bondage, freedom. I walk in that liberty.

Father, I praise You with joyful lips. I am ever
filled and stimulated with the Holy Spirit. I
speak out in psalms and hymns making melody
with all my heart to You, Lord. My happy heart
is a good medicine and my cheerful mind works

healing. The light in my eyes rejoices the hearts of others, and I have a good report. My countenance radiates the joy of the Lord.

Father, I thank You that I bear much prayer fruit. I ask in Jesus' name, and I will receive so that my joy (gladness, delight) may be full, complete, and overflowing. The joy of the Lord is my strength, and I count it all joy, all strength, when I encounter tests or trials of any sort because I am strong in You, Father.

Your right hand has defeated Satan, so I am not moved by adverse circumstances. I have the victory in the name of Jesus. I have been made the righteousness of God in Christ Jesus. I dwell in the Kingdom of God and have peace and joy in the Holy Spirit! Praise the Lord!

Scripture References

Psalms 63:5; 118:24; 144:15

Philippians 3:1; 4:4,8

Zephaniah 3:17

Isaiah 51:11

2 Corinthians 3:17; 5:7,21

James 1:2,25

Ephesians 1:22; 5:18,19; 6:10

Proverbs 15:13,30; 17:22

John 15:7,8; 16:23

Nehemiah 8:10

1 John 5:4

Romans 14:17

6

To Walk in God's Wisdom and His Perfect Will

Lord and God, You are worthy to receive glory, honor, and power, for You created all things, and by Your will they were created and have their being. You adopted me as Your child through Jesus Christ, in accordance with Your pleasure and will. I am active in sharing my faith, so that I will have a full understanding of every good thing I have in Christ.

Father, I ask You for complete understanding of what You want to do in my life, and I ask You to make me wise with spiritual wisdom. Then the way I live will always honor and please You, and I will continually do good, kind things for others. All the while, I will learn to know You better and better.

I roll my works upon You, Lord, and You make my thoughts agreeable to Your will, and so my plans are established and succeed. You direct my steps and make them sure. I understand and firmly grasp what the will of the Lord is; for I am not vague, thoughtless, or foolish. I stand firm and mature in spiritual growth, convinced and fully assured in everything willed by God.

Father, You have destined and appointed me to come progressively to know Your will — that is to perceive, to recognize more strongly and clearly, and to become better and more intimately acquainted with Your will. I thank You, Father, for the Holy Spirit Who abides permanently in me, and Who guides me into all the truth and speaks whatever He hears from You, announcing and declaring to me the things that are to come. I have the mind of Christ and hold the thoughts, feelings, and purposes of His heart.

So, Father, I enter into that blessed rest by adhering to, trusting in, and relying on You in the name of Jesus. Hallelujah!

Scripture References

Revelation 4:11 NIV

Ephesians 1:5 NIV;
   5:16 AMP

Colossians 1:9,10 NLT

Proverbs 16:3,9 AMP

Colossians 4:12 AMP

Acts 22:14

1 Corinthians 2:16 AMP

Hebrews 4:10

7

To Walk in Love

Father, in Jesus' name, thank You that the Holy Spirit has poured forth Your love into my heart. The love of and for You, Father, has been perfected and completed in me, and perfect love casts out all fear.

Father, because I am a partaker of Your divine nature, I commit to walk in Your kind of love. I endure long; I am patient with my children and kind to them. I am never envious and never boil over with jealousy. I am not boastful or vainglorious, and I do not display myself haughtily. I am not rude and unmannerly, and I do not act unbecomingly. I do not insist on my own rights or my own way; for I am not self-seeking, touchy, fretful, or resentful.

I take no account of an evil done to me and pay no attention to a suffered wrong. I do not rejoice at injustice and unrighteousness, but I rejoice when right and truth prevail. I bear up under anything and everything that comes. I am ever ready to believe the best of others. My hopes for my children's future are fadeless under all circumstances. I endure everything without weakening, because Your love in me never fails.

Father, my love abounds yet more and more in knowledge and in all judgment. I approve things that are excellent. I am sincere and without offense till the day of Christ, filled with the fruits of righteousness.

I am rooted deep in and founded securely on love, knowing that You are strengthening me, and nothing can separate me from Your love, which is in Christ Jesus my Lord. Thank You, Father, in Jesus' precious name. Amen.

———

Scripture References

Romans 5:5; 12:14 AMP;	Matthew 5:44
8:31,39	Philippians 1:9-11
1 John 2:5; 4:18	John 13:34
1 Corinthians 3:6 KJV;	Daniel 1:9 AMP
13:4-8 AMP	Ephesians 3:17 AMP

8

To Walk in Forgiveness

Father, in the name of Jesus, I make a fresh commitment to You to live in peace and harmony, not only with the other brothers and sisters of Christ, but also with my friends, associates, neighbors, and family.

Father, I repent of holding on to bad feelings toward others. I bind myself to godly repentance and loose bitterness, resentment, envying, strife, and unkindness in any form from my heart and mind. Father, I ask Your forgiveness for the sin of _____. By faith, I receive it, having assurance that I am cleansed from all unrighteousness through Jesus Christ. I ask You to forgive and release all who have wronged and hurt me. I forgive and release them. Deal with them in Your mercy and loving-kindness.

From this moment on, I purpose to walk in love, to seek peace, to live in agreement, and to conduct myself toward others in a manner that is pleasing to You. I know that I have right standing with You, and Your ears are attentive to my prayers.

The Holy Ghost, Who is given to me, has poured the love of God into my heart. I believe that love flows forth into the lives of my children and everyone I know, that we may be filled with and abound in the fruits of righteousness that bring glory and honor unto You, Lord, in Jesus' name. So be it!

Scripture References

Romans 5:5; 12:10,16-18

Philippians 1:11 AMP; 2:2

Ephesians 4:27,31,32

John 1:9

Mark 11:25

1 Peter 3:8,11,12

Colossians 1:10

9

To Watch What You Say

Father, I turn from idle words and foolishly speaking things that are contrary to my true desires. The tongue defiles, sets on fire the course of nature; it is set on fire of hell.

I renounce, reject, and repent of every word that has ever proceeded out of my mouth against You, God, and Your operation. I cancel its power and dedicate my mouth to speak excellent and right things. I speak words of wisdom that are gentle and reasonable, over-flowing with mercy and blessings.

Because You made me the righteousness of God in Christ Jesus, I set the course of my life for obedience, abundance, wisdom, health, and joy. O Lord, set a guard over my mouth; keep watch over the door of my lips. Then the words of my mouth and my deeds shall show forth Your righteousness and Your salvation all of my days. I purpose to guard my mouth and my tongue that I might keep my family from calamity.

Father, Your words, which are spirit and life, are top priority to me. The Word dwells in me richly in all wisdom. I speak Your words releasing Your ability within me. They are alive and working in me. So I boldly say that my words are words of faith, words of power, words of love, and words of life, producing good things in my life and in the lives of others, in Jesus' name.

Scripture References

Ephesians 4:27; 5:4	2 Corinthians 5:21
2 Timothy 2:16	John 6:63
James 1:6; 3:6	Colossians 3:16
Proverbs 4:23; 8:6,7; 21:23	Philemon 6

10

To Live Free From Worry

Father, I thank You that I am delivered from the power of darkness and translated into the Kingdom of Your dear Son. In the name of Jesus, I live free from worry, for the law of the Spirit of life in Christ Jesus has made me free from the law of sin and death.

I humble myself under Your mighty hand casting the whole of my cares *(name them)* — all my anxieties, worries, and concerns on You. Thank You for affectionately and watchfully caring for me and sustaining me. You will never allow the consistently righteous to be moved — made to slip, fall, or fail!

Father, I delight myself in You, and You perfect that which concerns me. I cast down imaginations (reasonings) and every high thing that exalts itself against the knowledge of You,

and bring into captivity every thought to the
obedience of Christ. I lay aside every weight
and the sin of worry, which does try so easily to
beset me. I run with patience the race that is set
before me, looking unto Jesus, the Author and
Finisher of my faith.

Father, You are able to keep that which I have
committed unto You. I think on (fix my mind
on) those things that are true, honest, just, pure,
lovely, of good report, virtuous, and deserving of
praise. I guard my heart and will not let it be
troubled. I abide in Your Word, and Your Word
abides in me. I look into the perfect law of
liberty and continue therein, being not a
forgetful hearer, but a doer of the Word and
thus blessed in my doing!

Thank You, Father. I am carefree. I walk in
that peace which passes all understanding, in
Jesus' name!

Scripture References

Colossians 1:13

Romans 8:2

1 Peter 5:6,7 AMP

Psalms 37:4,5; 55:22;
  138:8

2 Corinthians 10:5

Hebrews 12:1,2

2 Timothy 1:12

Philippians 4:6,8

John 14:1; 15:7

James 1:22-25

11

Provision: "Give Us This Day Our Daily Bread"

Father, You provide food, clothing, and shelter for my family, and I am ever grateful. In the name of Jesus, I am not uneasy (anxious and worried) about my life, what we shall eat and what we shall drink, or what we shall put on. Life is greater [in quality] than food, and the body [far above and more excellent] than clothing.

The bread of idleness [gossip, discontent, and self-pity] I will not eat. Father, thank You for liberally supplying (filling to the full) our every need according to Your riches in glory in Christ Jesus.

In the name of Jesus, I shall not live by bread alone, but by every word that proceeds from the mouth of God. Your words were found, and I did eat them. They were joy to me, and the rejoicing of my heart.

Jesus, the Word — the Living Bread, became flesh and dwelt among us, and I have beheld His glory.

Thank You, Father, in the name of Jesus, for spiritual bread — manna from heaven.

Scripture References

Matthew 4:4 KJV;
  6:9-11,25 AMP
Jeremiah 15:16 AMP
Proverbs 31:27 AMP

Philippians 4:19 AMP
Psalm 37:25
John 1:14 KJV;
  6:48-51 AMP

12

Strength To Overcome Cares and Burdens

Father, I submit to Your will. In the name of Jesus, I resist the devil when he tries to pressure me with the cares of the world. I draw near to You, my Beloved, and You draw near to me. Jesus, I come to You, for I am heavy laden and overburdened with many things. You cause me to rest — You ease, relieve, and refresh my soul. I take Your yoke upon me, and I learn of You; for You are gentle (meek) and humble (lowly) in heart, and I will find rest — relief, ease, refreshment, recreation, and blessed quiet — for my soul. For Your yoke is wholesome (easy) — not harsh, hard, sharp, or pressing — but comfortable, gracious, and pleasant, and Your burden is light and easy to be borne.

Why are you cast down, O my inner self? And why should you moan over me and be disquieted within me?

I cast my burden on You, Lord, [releasing the weight of it] and You will sustain me; I thank You that You will never allow me, the [consistently] righteous, to be moved — made to slip, fall, or fail.

In the name of Jesus, I withstand the devil. I am firm in my faith [against his onset] — rooted, established, strong, immovable, and determined. I cease from [the weariness and pain] of human labor, and am zealous, exerting myself and striving diligently to enter into the rest [of God] — to know and experience it for myself.

Father, I thank You that Your presence goes with me, and that You give me rest. I am still and rest in You, Lord; I wait for You and patiently stay myself upon You. I will not fret myself, nor shall I let my heart be troubled, neither shall I let it be afraid. I hope in You, God, and wait expectantly for You; for I shall yet praise You, for You are the help of my countenance and my God.

Scripture References (AMP)

Psalms 37:7; 42:11;
  55:22; 127:1
James 4:6,7
Matthew 11:28-30

1 Peter 5:9
Hebrews 4:10,11
Exodus 33:14
John 14:27b

13

Conquering the Thought Life

Father, in the name of Jesus, I take authority over my thought life. Even though I walk (live) in the flesh, I am not carrying on my warfare according to the flesh and using mere human weapons. The weapons of my warfare are not physical, but they are mighty before God for the overthrow and destruction of strongholds. I refute arguments, theories, reasonings, and every proud and lofty thing that sets itself up against the (true) knowledge of You; and I lead every thought and purpose away captive into the obedience of Christ, the Messiah, the Anointed One.

With my soul, with every thought and purpose in life I will bless You, Lord. My mind will not wander out of the presence of God. My life glorifies the Father — spirit, soul, and body. I take no account of the evil done to me — I pay no attention to a suffered wrong. It holds no place in my thought life. I am ever ready to believe the best of every person. I gird up the loins of my mind, setting my mind on what is above — the higher things — not on the things that are on the earth.

Whatever is true, worthy of reverence, honorable and seemly, whatever is just and pure, whatever is lovely and lovable, whatever is kind, winsome, and gracious, if there is any virtue and excellence, if there is anything worthy of praise, I will think on, weigh, and take account of these things — I fix my mind on them.

I have the mind of Christ, the Messiah, and do hold the thoughts (feelings and purposes) of His heart. In the name of Jesus, I practice what I have learned, received, heard, and seen in Christ, and model my way of living on it, and the God of peace — of untroubled, undisturbed well-being — will be with me.

———

Scripture References (AMP)

2 Corinthians 10:3-5   1 Peter 1:13
Psalm 103:1   Colossians 3:2
1 Corinthians 2:16;   Philippians 4:8,9
    6:20; 13:5,7

14

Godly Wisdom in the Affairs of Life

Father, I ask in faith to be filled with the knowledge of Your will in all wisdom and spiritual understanding. I incline my ear unto wisdom and apply my heart to understanding.

In the name of Jesus, I receive skill, godly wisdom, and instruction. I discern and comprehend the words of understanding and insight. As a person of understanding, I acquire skill and attain sound counsels [so that I may be able to steer my course rightly].

Wisdom guards me. I love, highly prize, and exalt her; she will bring me to honor because I embrace her. She gives to my head a wreath of gracefulness, a crown of beauty and glory. Length of days is in her right hand, and in her left hand are riches and honor.

Jesus has been made unto me wisdom, and in Him are all the treasures of [divine] wisdom and [all the riches of spiritual] knowledge and enlightenment. God has hidden away sound and godly wisdom and stored it up for me, for I am the righteousness of God in Christ Jesus.

When I am walking in paths of uprightness, my steps shall not be hampered — my path will be clear and open; and when I run I shall not stumble. I take fast hold of instruction and do not let her go; I guard her, for she is my life. I let my eyes look right on [with fixed purpose], and my gaze is straight before me. I consider well the path of my feet, and I let all my ways be established and ordered aright.

Father, in the name of Jesus, I look carefully to how I walk! I live purposefully, worthily, and accurately — not as unwise and witless, but as a wise, sensible, intelligent person. I make the very most of my time — buying up every opportunity.

Scripture References

Proverbs 1:2-5; 2:2,7; 3:16;
    4:6,8,9,11-13,25,26 AMP

James 1:5,6

Colossians 1:9

2 Corinthians 5:21

1 Corinthians 1:30

Colossians 2:3 AMP

Ephesians 5:15,16 AMP

15

The Setting of Proper Priorities

Father, I ask You to help me establish priorities. Your grace is sufficient for every situation. Your strength comes into its own in my weakness. I am living purposefully, worthily, and accurately as a wise, sensible, intelligent person.

You have given me a seven-day week: six days to work and the seventh to rest. Help me make the most of the time [buying up each opportunity]. Help me plan my day and stay focused on my assignments.

In the name of Jesus, I smash warped philosophies, tear down barriers erected against the truth of God, and fit every loose thought, emotion, and impulse into the structure of life shaped by Christ. I clear my mind of every obstruction and build a life of obedience into maturity.

Father, I plan the way I want to live —organizing my efforts, scheduling my activities, and budgeting my time — but You alone enable me to live it. Jesus, You want me to relax, to not be preoccupied with getting, so I can respond to God's giving. I know You, Father God, and how You work. I steep my life in God-reality, God-initiative, and God-provisions.

Father, I cast all my cares, worries, and concerns over on You, that I might be well-balanced (temperate, sober of mind), vigilant, and cautious at all times. I tune my ears to the word of wisdom, set my heart on a life of understanding, and make insight my priority. My life is complete in Christ.

Father, You sent Jesus that I might know You and have abundant life. My relationships with You and others are more important than anything else here in this life. Amen.

Scripture References

Matthew 6:31-33 MESSAGE;
  11:29 MESSAGE, AMP
Ephesians 5:15,16 AMP
2 Corinthians 10:5,6
  MESSAGE
Colossians 2:10

Genesis 2:2 NIV
Proverbs 2:3; 16:3,9
  MESSAGE
1 Peter 5:7,8 AMP
John 10:10

16

Knowing God's Will

Father, thank You for instructing me in the way that I should go and for guiding me with Your eye. I thank You for revealing Your will, Your plan, and Your purpose for my life. I do hear the voice of the Good Shepherd, for I know You and follow You. You lead me in the paths of righteousness for Your name's sake.

As I follow You, my path is becoming clearer, growing brighter and brighter until it reaches the full light of day.

Thank You, Father, that Jesus was made unto me wisdom. I am trusting You with all my heart. I look to You for understanding, and in all my ways I acknowledge You, and You are directing my paths. In Jesus' name, I am not confused about Your will for my life.

Scripture References

Psalms 16:11; 23:3; 32:8

John 10:3,4

Proverbs 3:5,6; 4:18

Ephesians 5:19

1 Corinthians 1:30;
  14:33

17

The New Creation Marriage

Father, in the name of Jesus, I thank You for my husband who seeks first Your kingdom and Your righteousness, Your way of doing and being right. Together we are growing up in all things, reaching our full potential. I thank You for meeting our innermost needs as we build a godly home, fulfilling Your purpose for the building up of Your kingdom. When I speak I have something worthwhile to say, and I say it with kindness. When others see our love for one another, they will believe that You sent Jesus to give them eternal life.

Scripture References

Ephesians 1:4,6,8;
   5:22,25-30,33 AMP
2 Corinthians 3:6;
   5:17,18
Philippians 2:15 AMP

1 Peter 2:23 AMP
Matthew 19:5,6 AMP
1 Corinthians 11:7 AMP
Proverbs 31:11,12 AMP

18

Harmonious Marriage

Father, Your love is shed abroad in our hearts by the Holy Ghost, Who is given to us. Because You are in us, Your love reigns supreme, is displayed in full expression, enfolding and knitting us together in truth, making us perfect for every good work to do Your will, working in us that which is pleasing in Your sight.

We live and conduct our marriage and ourselves honorably and becomingly. We esteem it as precious, worthy, and of great price. We commit ourselves to live in mutual harmony and accord with one another delighting in each other, being of the same mind and united in spirit.

Father, we are gentle, compassionate, courteous, tenderhearted, and humble-minded. We seek peace, and it keeps our hearts in quietness and assurance. Because we follow after love and dwell in peace, our prayers are not hindered in any way, in the name of Jesus. We are heirs together of the grace of God.

Our marriage grows stronger day by day in the bond of unity because it is founded on Your Word and rooted and grounded in Your love. Father, we thank You for the performance of it, in Jesus' name.

Scripture References

Romans 5:5	Ephesians 3:17,18; 4:32
Philippians 1:9;	1 Peter 3:7
2:2,13; 4:7	Isaiah 32:17
Colossians 1:10; 3:14	Jeremiah 1:12

19

The Unborn Child

Father, in Jesus' name, I thank You for my unborn child who is a gift from You. You are watching over my child who is being formed in my womb, healthy and complete.

You have known my child since conception and know the path he/she will take with his/her life. I ask Your blessing upon him/her and stand in faith for his/her salvation through Jesus Christ.

When You created man and woman, You called them blessed and crowned them with glory and honor. It is in You, Father, that my child will live and move, and have his/her being. He/she is Your offspring and will come to worship and praise You.

Heavenly Father, I thank and praise You for the great things You have done and are continuing

to do. I am in awe at the miracle of life You
have placed inside of me. Thank You! Amen.

Scripture References

Psalms 8:5; 91:1; 127:3	Matthew 18:18
Genesis 1:26	John 14:13
Jeremiah 1:5	Galatians 3:13
2 Peter 3:9	1 John 3:8
Acts 17:28,29	

20

The Children

Father, in Jesus' name, I am a virtuous woman of might and power proclaiming Your Word over my children, surrounding them with prayers of faith. My children are disciples of Christ, taught of the Lord, and obedient to Your will. Great is their peace and undisturbed composure, for You contend for, protect, and ease them.

I cast the care of my children over on You, knowing that You are able to guard and keep them. You are more than enough!

In the name of Jesus, I bind my children — spirit, soul, and body — to obedience because this is just and right. They honor, esteem, and value as precious their parents; therefore, all will be well with them and they will live long on earth. They choose life and love You, and obey

Your voice; for You are their life and the length of their days.

My children are the head and not the tail, above only and not beneath. They are blessed coming in and going out. You give Your angels charge over them to accompany, defend, and preserve them in all their ways. You are their refuge and fortress, their glory and the lifter of their heads.

We will not provoke, irritate, or fret our children. We will not break or wound their spirits, but we will rear them tenderly in the training, discipline, counsel, and admonition of the Lord. We will train them in the way they should go, and when they are old they will not depart from it.

O Lord, out of the mouths of babes and unweaned infants You have established strength because of Your foes, that You might silence the enemy and the avenger. The enemy is turned back from my children, in the name of Jesus! They increase in wisdom and in favor with God and man.

Scripture References

Jeremiah 1:12

Isaiah 49:25; 54:13

Psalms 3:3; 8:1,2; 91:2,11

Colossians 3:21

Deuteronomy 28:3,6,13;
  30:19,20

Ephesians 6:1-4

1 Peter 5:7

2 Timothy 1:12

Proverbs 22:6

Luke 2:52

21

Children at School

Father, I make up a wall and stand in the gap before You on behalf of my children as they pursue their education. You are effectually at work creating within them the power and desire to please You. They are the head and not the tail, above and not beneath, finding favor, good understanding, and high esteem in the sight of God, their teachers, and their classmates. I ask You to give them wisdom and understanding as knowledge is presented to them in all fields of study and endeavor.

Father, thank You for giving them an appreciation for education and helping them to understand that You are the Source of all knowledge. They have the appetite of the diligent, and they are abundantly supplied with educational resources; their thoughts are those of the steadily diligent, which tend only to achievement. They are growing in wisdom and knowledge. I will not cease to pray for them, asking that they be filled with the knowledge of Your will, bearing fruit in every good work.

Father, thank You that my children dwell in the secret place of the Most High. They trust and find their refuge in You and stand rooted and grounded in Your love. They shall not be led astray by philosophies of men and teaching that is contrary to truth. You are their Shield and Buckler, protecting them from attacks or threats. Thank You for the angels who accompany, defend, and preserve them in all their ways of obedience and service. They are established in Your love, which drives out all fear.

I pray that their teachers will be godly men and women of integrity, with understanding hearts and wisdom walking in the ways of piety and virtue, revering Your holy name. Amen.

Scripture References

Philippians 2:13	Colossians 1:9,10
Deuteronomy 28:1,2,13	1 Kings 4:29
Proverbs 1:4,7; 3:4,13; 4:5	Daniel 1:4
Ephesians 1:17; 3:17; 4:14	Matthew 18:18
Psalms 91:1,2,3-11; 112:8	James 1:5

22

The Home

Father, in the name of Jesus, I am a woman of confidence. My family and I are blessed with all spiritual blessings in Christ Jesus. Jesus has been made unto me wisdom.

Through skillful and godly wisdom is my house (my life, my home, my family) built, and by understanding it is established on a sound and good foundation. And by knowledge shall the chambers (of its every area) be filled with all precious and pleasant riches — great priceless treasure. My house shall stand. Prosperity and welfare are in my house, in the name of Jesus.

My house is securely built. It is founded on a rock — revelation knowledge of Your Word, Father. Jesus is my Cornerstone — the Lord of my household. Whatever may be our task, we work at it heartily as something done for You,

Lord, and not for men. We love each other with the God kind of love, and we dwell in peace. My home is deposited into Your charge, entrusted to Your protection and care.

Father, I give myself to my God-called work, and I am successful in my effort in Jesus' name. Hallelujah!

Scripture References

Ephesians 1:3	Luke 6:48
Proverbs 12:7;	Acts 4:11; 16:31; 20:32
24:3,4 AMP	Philippians 2:10,11
Proverbs 15:6	Colossians 3:14,15,23
Psalm 112:3	Joshua 24:15

23

Prosperity

Father, You are a very present help in trouble, and You are more than enough. You are faithful to supply all my need according to Your riches in glory by Christ Jesus.

(If you have not been giving tithes and offerings, include this statement of repentance in your prayer.) Forgive me for robbing You in tithes and offerings. I repent and purpose to bring all my tithes into the storehouse that there may be food in Your house. Thank You for wise financial counselors and teachers who are teaching me the principles of good stewardship.

Lord of hosts, You said, "Try Me now in this, and I will open the windows of heaven and pour out for you such blessing that there will not be room enough to receive it." You will rebuke the devourer for my sake, and my heart is filled with thanksgiving.

Lord, my God, You are the One Who gives me the power to get wealth that You may establish Your covenant. In the name of Jesus, I worship You only; I have no others gods before me.

You are able to make all grace — every favor and earthly blessing — come to me in abundance, so that I am always, and in all circumstances, furnished in abundance for every good work and charitable donation. Amen.

Scripture References

Psalm 56:1

Philippians 4:19

Malachi 3:8-12

Deuteronomy 8:18,19

2 Corinthians 9:8 AMP

24

Dedication for Your Tithes

I profess this day unto the Lord God that I have come into the inheritance that the Lord swore to give me. I am in the land that You provided for me in Jesus Christ, the Kingdom of Almighty God. I was a sinner serving Satan; he was my god. But I called upon the name of Jesus; You heard my cry and brought me into the Kingdom of Your dear Son.

Jesus, my Lord and High Priest, I bring the firstfruits of my income to You and worship the Lord my God with them.

I rejoice in all the good that You have given to us. I hearken to the voice of the Lord my God and do according to all that He commands me. Now look down from Your holy habitation and bless me as You said in Your Word. I thank You, Father, in Jesus' name.

Scripture References

Deuteronomy 26:1,3,10,
 11,14,15 AMP

Ephesians 2:1-5

Colossians 1:13

Hebrews 3:1,7,8

25

Victory in a Healthy Lifestyle

Father, I am a woman of power and might; Jesus is Lord over my spirit, soul, and body. I praise You because I am fearfully and wonderfully made. Your works are wonderful; I know that full well.

Lord, thank You for declaring Your plans for me — plans to prosper me and not to harm me, plans to give me hope and a future. I am renewing my mind to Your plans for a healthy lifestyle. You have abounded toward me in all prudence and wisdom. I give thought to my steps and to what I eat. Teach me knowledge and good judgment so that I might achieve and maintain the proper weight for my frame at my present age.

My body is for the Lord. So here's what I want to do with Your help, Father: take my everyday, ordinary life — my sleeping, eating, going-to-work, and walking-around life — and place it before You as an offering. Embracing what You do for me is the best thing I can do for You.

Christ the Messiah is magnified and receives glory and praise in this body of mine and is boldly exalted in my person. Thank You, Father, in Jesus' name! Hallelujah! Amen.

———

Scripture References

Psalms 119:66; 139:14   Romans 12:1 MESSAGE

Jeremiah 29:11   Philippians 1:20 AMP

Proverbs 14:15

26

Health and Healing

Father, I come before You believing that it is Your will to heal me from this infirmity.

My body is the temple of the Holy Spirit, and I seek truth that will make me free — both spiritual and natural (good eating habits, medications if necessary, and appropriate rest and exercise). You bought me at a price, and I desire to glorify You in my spirit and my body — they both belong to You.

Thank You, Father, for sending Your Word to heal me and deliver me from all my destructions. Jesus, You bore my griefs (pains) and carried my sorrows (sickness). You were pierced through for my transgressions and crushed for my iniquities; the chastening for my well-being fell upon You, and by Your stripes I am healed.

Father, I give attention to Your words and incline my ear to Your sayings. I will not let them depart from my sight, but I will keep them in the midst of my heart, for they are life and health to my whole body.

Since the Spirit of Him Who raised Jesus from the dead dwells in me, He Who raised Christ from the dead will also give life to my mortal body through His Spirit, Who dwells in me.

I bless You, Lord, with all that is within me. I thank You for forgiving all my iniquities and healing all my diseases. Thank You that I will prosper and be in health, even as my soul prospers. Amen.

Scripture References

James 5:15 NKJV

1 Corinthians 6:19,20

Psalms 103:3-5 NASB; 107:20

John 1:14

Isaiah 53:4,5 NASB

Proverbs 4:21,22 NASB

Romans 8:11 NKJV

3 John 2

27

Safety

Father, in the name of Jesus, I thank You that I dwell in the secret place of the Most High and that I remain stable and fixed under the shadow of the Almighty, Whose power no foe can withstand.

Father, You are my refuge and my fortress. No evil shall befall me — no accident shall overtake me — nor any plague or calamity come near my home. You give Your angels special charge over me, to accompany and defend and preserve me in all my ways of obedience and service. They are encamped around about me.

Father, You are my confidence, firm and strong, keeping my foot from being caught in a trap or hidden danger. Father, You give me safety and ease — Jesus is my safety!

Traveling — As I go, I say, "Let me pass over to the other side," and I have what I say. I walk on my way securely and in confident trust, for my heart and mind are firmly fixed and stayed on You, and I am kept in perfect peace.

Sleeping — Father, I sing for joy upon my bed because You sustain me. In peace I lie down and sleep, for You alone, Lord, make me dwell in safety. I lie down, and I am not afraid. My sleep is sweet, for You give blessings to me in sleep. Thank You, Father, in Jesus' name. Amen.

Continue to feast and meditate upon all of Psalm 91 for yourself and your loved ones!

Scripture References

Psalms 3:5; 34:7; 112:7;   Jeremiah 1:12
   127:2; 149:5   Proverbs 3:23,24,26 AMP
Psalms 4:8; 91:1,2,10,11   Isaiah 26:3; 49:25
   AMP   Mark 4:35 AMP

28

Peaceful Sleep

Father, thank You for the angels that encamp around those who fear You. You deliver us and keep us safe. The angels excel in strength and heed the voice of Your Word. You give Your angels charge over me, to keep me in all my ways.

I bring every thought, every imagination, and every dream into the captivity and obedience of Jesus Christ. Father, I thank You that even as I sleep my heart counsels me and reveals to me Your purpose and plan. Thank You for sweet sleep, for You promised Your beloved sweet sleep. My heart is glad, my spirit rejoices, and my body and soul rest and confidently dwell in safety. Amen.

Scripture References

Psalms 16:7-9; 91:11;   Matthew 16:19; 18:18
  103:20; 127:2   2 Corinthians 10:5
Proverbs 3:24

29

Victory Over Pride

Father, I submit my will to You. In the name of Jesus, I resist the devil, and he will flee from me. I renounce every manifestation of pride in my life as sin; I repent and turn from it.

As an act of faith, I clothe myself with humility and receive Your grace. I humble myself under Your mighty hand, Lord, that You may exalt me in due time. I do not think of myself more highly than I ought; I do not have an exaggerated opinion of my own importance, but rate my ability with sober judgment, according to the degree of faith apportioned to me.

Proverbs 11:2 says, "When pride cometh, then cometh shame: but with the lowly is wisdom." Father, I set myself to resist pride when it comes. My desire is to be counted among the lowly, so I take on the attitude of a servant.

Father, You dwell with him who is of a contrite and humble spirit. You revive the spirit of the humble and revive the heart of the contrite ones. Thank You that the reward of humility and the reverent and worshipful fear of the Lord is riches, honor, and life.

In Jesus' name I pray. Amen.

———

Scripture References

Proverbs 6:16; 11:2; 21:4   Romans 12:3 AMP

Proverbs 22:4 AMP   Matthew 23:11

James 4:6,7   Isaiah 57:15

1 Peter 5:5,6

30

Victory Over Fear

Father, when I am afraid, I will put my confidence in You. Yes, I will trust Your promises. And since I trust You, what can mere man do to me?

You have not given me a spirit of timidity, but of power and love and discipline (sound judgment). Therefore, I am not ashamed of the testimony of my Lord. I have not received a spirit of slavery leading to fear again, but I have received a spirit of adoption as a daughter, by which I cry out, "Abba! Father!"

Jesus, You delivered me, who, through fear of death, had been living all my life as a slave to constant dread. I receive the gift You left to me — peace of mind and heart! And the peace You give isn't fragile like the peace the world gives. I cast away troubled thoughts, and I choose not to be afraid. I believe in God; I believe also in You.

Lord, You are my Light and my Salvation; You protect me from danger — whom shall I fear? When evil men come to destroy me, they will stumble and fall! Yes, though a mighty army marches against me, my heart shall know no fear! I am confident that You will save me.

Thank You, Holy Spirit, for bringing these things to my remembrance when fear arises. My trust is in You. In the name of Jesus, I pray. Amen.

Scripture References

Psalms 27:1-3; 56:3-5 TLB   Hebrews 2:15 TLB

2 Timothy 1:7,8 NASB   John 14:1,17 TLB

Romans 8:15 NASB

31

Victory Over Depression

Father, I lift my soul up to You. Meditating on the works of Your hands, I confidently put my trust in You. You will never leave me or forsake me. You are the help of my countenance and my God, my Deliverer from depression.

Lord, when I am bowed down You lift me up. In You I am strong and courageous. I trust You and bind my will to Your will in the name of Jesus.

Father, You have thoughts and plans for my welfare and peace, not for disaster. In the name of Jesus, I loose wrong thought patterns from my mind. I cast down strongholds that have protected bad perceptions about who I am. I submit to You, Father, and resist fear, discouragement, self-pity, and depression. I will not give place to the devil by harboring resentment

and holding on to anger. I surround myself
with songs and shouts of deliverance from
depression, and will continue to be an over-
comer by the word of my testimony and the
blood of the Lamb.

Father, I thank You that I have been given a
spirit of power, love, and a calm and well-
balanced mind. I have discipline and self-
control. I have the mind of Christ and hold the
thoughts, feelings, and purposes of His heart.
Thank You for a fresh mental and spiritual attitude, for I am constantly renewed in the spirit
of my mind with Your Word, Father.

Therefore, I brace up and reinvigorate and cut
through and make firm and straight paths for
my feet — safe and upright and happy paths
that go in the right direction. I arise from the
depression and prostration in which circumstances have kept me. I rise to new life. I shine
and am radiant with the glory of the Lord.

Thank You, Father, in Jesus' name, that I am
set free from every evil work. I praise You that
the joy of the Lord is my strength and stronghold! Hallelujah!

Scripture References

Isaiah 26:3; 35:3,4;
   50:10; 54:14

Isaiah 60:1 AMP

Psalms 9:9,10;
   31:24 AMP

Psalm 146:8

Jeremiah 29:11-13 AMP

John 14:27 AMP

James 4:7

Ephesians 4:23,24 AMP;
   4:27

Luke 4:18,19

2 Timothy 1:7 AMP

1 Corinthians 2:16

Philippians 2:5

Hebrews 12:12,13 AMP

Galatians 1:4

Nehemiah 8:10 AMP

32

Deliverance From Habits

Father, I believe in my heart and say with my mouth that Jesus is Lord of my life. Since all truth is in Jesus, I strip myself of my former nature [put off and discard my old, unrenewed self]. Father, this habit of _____ is not helpful (good for me, expedient, and profitable when considered with other things). In the name of Jesus I declare my freedom from slavery to wrong habits and behaviors.

Father, Your Word exposes the wrong thought patterns that have driven me to continue acting out in ways that are contrary to Your Word. I desire to be continually filled with, and controlled by, the Holy Spirit.

Thank You, Father, for translating me into the Kingdom of Your dear Son. Now I am Your garden under cultivation. In the name of Jesus, I throw all spoiled virtue and cancerous evil into the garbage. In simple humility, I purpose to let You, my Gardener, landscape me with the Word, making a salvation-garden of my life.

I put on the full armor of God: the helmet of salvation; loins girded with truth; feet shod with the preparation of the gospel of peace; the shield of faith; and the Sword of the Spirit, which is the Word of God. Thus, I stand against all Satan's strategies, deceits, and fiery darts, in Jesus' name. I discipline my body and subdue it. With every temptation I choose the way of escape that You provide. Greater is He that is in me than he that is in the world.

Thank You, Lord. I praise You that I am growing spiritually and that Your engrafted Word is saving my soul. I strip away the old nature with its habits, and I put on the new person created in Christ Jesus. Hallelujah! Amen.

Scripture References

Romans 10:9,10   James 1:21 MESSAGE
Ephesians 4:21,22   1 Corinthians 10:13
1 Corinthians 3:9; 6:12 AMP   1 John 4:4

33

Spirit-Controlled Life

Father, I pray for all saints, declaring that our hearts and minds are ready to receive instruction from Your ministers who are equipping us for the work of ministry, the edifying of the Body of Christ. Bring us to the unity of faith and knowledge of the Son of God, to the measure of the stature of the fullness of Christ.

Father, there is now no condemnation to those who walk according to the Spirit because, through Christ Jesus, the law of the Spirit of life set us free from the law of sin and death. Grant us the grace to live the life of the Spirit. Father, You condemned sin in the flesh [subdued, overcame, deprived it] of its power over us. Now the righteous and just requirement of the Law is fully met in us who live and move in the ways of the Spirit.

We purpose to live according to the Spirit, and we are controlled by the desires of the Spirit. We set our minds on and seek those things which gratify the Holy Spirit. We no longer live the life of the flesh; we live the life of the Spirit. The Holy Spirit of God really dwells within us, directing and controlling us.

On the authority of Your Word, we declare that we are more than conquerors and are gaining a surpassing victory through Jesus, Who loves us. We refuse to let ourselves be overcome with evil, but we will overcome and master evil with good. We have on the full armor of light, clothed with the Lord Jesus Christ, the Messiah, and make no provision for indulging the flesh.

May we always be doers of God's Word. We have God's wisdom, and we draw it forth with prayer. We are peace-loving, full of compassion and good fruits. We are free from doubts, wavering, and insincerity. We are subject to God, our Father.

We are strong in the Lord and the power of His might. We take our stand against the devil and resist him; and he flees from us. We draw close to God, and God draws close to us.

In Christ, we are filled with the Godhead: Father, Son, and Holy Spirit. Jesus is our Lord!

———

Scripture References

Romans 8:2,4,9,14, 31,37 AMP

Romans 12:21; 13:12,14

James 1:22; 4:7,8

James 3:17 AMP

Hebrews 13:5

Colossians 2:10

34

Finding Favor With Others

A Prayer of Intercession

Father, in the name of Jesus, You make Your face to shine upon and enlighten _____ and are gracious (kind, merciful, and giving favor) to him/her. _____ is the head and not the tail. _____ is above only and not beneath.

Thank You for favor for _____, who seeks Your Kingdom and Your righteousness and diligently seeks good. _____ is a blessing to You, Lord, and is a blessing to *(name them: family, neighbors, business associates, etc.)*. Grace (favor) is with _____, who loves the Lord Jesus in sincerity. _____ extends favor, honor, and love to *(names)*. _____ is flowing in Your love, Father. You are pouring out upon _____ the spirit of favor.

You crown him/her with glory and honor, for he/she is Your child — Your workmanship.

_____ is a success today. _____ is someone very special with You, Lord. _____ is growing in the Lord — waxing strong in spirit. Father, You give _____ knowledge and skill in all learning and wisdom.

You bring _____ to find favor, compassion, and loving-kindness with _____ *(names)*. _____ obtains favor in the sight of all who look upon him/her this day, in the name of Jesus. _____ is filled with Your fullness — rooted and grounded in love. You are doing exceeding abundantly above all that _____ asks or thinks, for Your mighty power is taking over in _____.

Thank You, Father, that _____ is well-favored by You and by man, in Jesus' name!

Scripture References

Numbers 6:25

Deuteronomy 28:13

Matthew 6:33

Proverbs 11:27

Ephesians 2:10;
   3:19,20; 6:24

Luke 6:38

Zechariah 12:10

Psalm 8:5

Luke 2:40

Daniel 1:9,17

Esther 2:15,17

35

American Government

Father, in Jesus' name, we give thanks for the United States and its government. We intercede for our leaders and their families, all those in authority over us in any way. We pray that the Spirit of the Lord rests upon them.

We believe that skillful and godly wisdom has entered into the heart of our president and knowledge is pleasant to him. Discretion watches over him; understanding keeps him and delivers him from evil.

Father, we ask that You encircle the president with people who make their hearts and ears attentive to godly counsel and do right in Your sight. We believe You cause them to be people of integrity who are obedient concerning us that we may lead a quiet and peaceable life in all godliness and honesty. We pray that the upright shall dwell in our government, that leaders blameless and complete in Your sight shall remain but the wicked shall be cut off from our government and the treacherous shall be rooted out.

Your Word declares that "blessed is the nation whose God is the Lord" (Ps. 33:12). We receive Your blessing. Father, You are our Refuge and Stronghold in times of trouble (high cost, destitution, and desperation). So we declare with our mouths that Your people dwell safely in this land, and we *prosper* abundantly. We are more than conquerors through Christ Jesus!

It is written in Your Word that the heart of the king is in the hand of the Lord, and You turn it whichever way You desire. We believe the heart of our leader is in Your hand and that his decisions are directed of the Lord.

We give thanks unto You that the good news of the Gospel is published in our land. The Word of the Lord prevails and grows mightily in the hearts and lives of the people. We give thanks for this land and the leaders You have given to us, in Jesus' name.

Jesus is Lord over the United States! Amen.

Scripture References

1 Timothy 2:1-3

Proverbs 2:10-12,21,22;
  21:1

Psalms 9:9; 33:12

Deuteronomy 28:10,11

Romans 8:37 AMP

Acts 12:24

Prayer of Salvation

God loves you—no matter who you are, no matter what your past. God loves you so much that He gave His one and only begotten Son for you. The Bible tells us, "…whoever believes in him shall not perish but have eternal life" (John 3:16 NIV). Jesus laid down His life and rose again so that we could spend eternity with Him in heaven and experience His absolute best on earth. If you would like to receive Jesus into your life, say the following prayer out loud and mean it from your heart.

Heavenly Father, I come to You admitting that I am a sinner. Right now, I choose to turn away from sin, and I ask You to cleanse me of all unrighteousness. I believe that Your Son, Jesus, died on the cross to take away my sins. I also believe that He rose again from the dead so that I might be forgiven of my sins and made righteous through faith in Him. I call upon the name of Jesus Christ to be the Savior and Lord of my life. Jesus, I choose to follow You and ask that You fill me with the power of the Holy Spirit. I declare that right now I am a child of God. I am free from sin and full of the righteousness of God. I am saved in Jesus' name. Amen.

If you prayed this prayer to receive Jesus Christ as your Savior for the first time, please contact us on the Web at **www.harrisonhouse.com** to receive a free book.

Or you may write to us at
Harrison House
P.O. Box 35035
Tulsa, Oklahoma 74153

About the Author

Germaine Griffin Copeland is the bestselling author of the *Prayers That Avail Much*® family of books. The books are now in several languages, and there are more than three million copies in print.

She is the daughter of the late Reverend A. H. "Buck" and Donnis Brock Griffin. Germaine lives with her husband, Everette, in Roswell, Georgia. They have four children, ten grandchildren, and five great-grandchildren.

MISSION STATEMENT
Word Ministries, Inc.

To motivate individuals to spiritual growth
and emotional wholeness,
encouraging them to become more deeply
and intimately acquainted
with the Father God
as they pray prayers that avail much.

You may contact Word Ministries by writing
Word Ministries, Inc.
38 Sloan Street
Roswell, Georgia 30075
or calling 770-518-1065
www.prayers.org

*Please include your testimonies
and praise reports when you write.*

Other Books by Germaine Copeland

A Call to Prayer

Prayers That Avail Much Commemorative Gift Edition

Prayers That Avail Much Commemorative Leather Edition

Prayers That Avail Much for Business

Prayers That Avail Much Volume 1

Prayers That Avail Much Volume 1 — mass market edition

Prayers That Avail Much Volume 2

Prayers That Avail Much Volume 2 — mass market edition

Prayers That Avail Much Volume 3

Prayers That Avail Much Volume 3 — mass market edition

Prayers That Avail Much for Men

Prayer That Avail Much for Dads — pocket edition

Prayers That Avail Much for Women

Prayers That Avail Much for Women — pocket edition

Prayers That Avail Much for Mothers — hardbound

Prayers That Avail Much for Mothers — paperback

Prayers That Avail Much for Moms — pocket edition

Prayers That Avail Much for Teens — hardbound

Prayers That Avail Much for Teens — mass market edition

Prayers That Avail Much for Graduates — pocket edition

Prayers That Avail Much for Kids

Prayers That Avail Much for Kids — Book 2

Prayers That Avail Much for the Workplace

Oraciones Con Poder — *Prayers That Avail Much*
(Spanish Edition)

More Prayers That Avail Much!

If this book has been a blessing to you, these dynamic prayers are available in their entirety in the clothbound edition of *Prayers That Avail Much*®. Check with your local bookstore or visit us at www.harrisonhouse.com. *Prayers That Avail Much for Women* — ISBN 1-57794-489-5

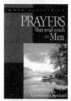

www.harrisonhouse.com

Fast. Easy. Convenient!

◆ New Book Information
◆ Look Inside the Book
◆ Press Releases
◆ Bestsellers

◆ Free E-News
◆ Author Biographies
◆ Upcoming Books
◆ Share Your Testimony

For the latest in book news and author information, please visit us on the Web at www.harrisonhouse.com. Get up-to-date pictures and details on all our powerful and life-changing products. Sign up for our e-mail newsletter, *Friends of the House,* and receive free monthly information on our authors and products including testimonials, author announcements, and more!

Harrison House—
Books That Bring Hope, Books That Bring Change

The Harrison House Vision

Proclaiming the truth and the power
Of the Gospel of Jesus Christ
With excellence;

Challenging Christians to
Live victoriously,
Grow spiritually,
Know God intimately.